The Lives of the Saints

Dale Harris's *The Lives of the Saints and Other Poems* offers a sweet introduction to the saints of the church. Each poem calls forth a longing in the reader to know more about the particular saint, as well as more about their loving faith in their living Lord. *Lives of the Saints* is a gift to evangelical Christians who are thirsty for the beautiful grittiness of cruciform faithfulness.

> Rev. David Schuchardt
> Lead Pastor, Northview Community Church
> Regina, SK

Harris masterfully offers the humanity of each saint alongside their saintly contribution to the church in their time. As a student of the history of Christian spirituality, I enjoyed seeing family names when I first thumbed through the collection, and then was engrossed by the humble request of poetry to slow down and savor the unique way in which each saint points to transcendent moments in life. Likewise, the "other poems" in this collection similarly weave observations about apparently mundane moments into divine encounters. I heartily recommend this collection of poetry that celebrates the great cloud of witnesses to the Christian faith.

> Amy Caswell Bratton
> Director of Operations & Publishing,
> New Leaf Network
> Author of *Witnesses of Perfect Love: Narratives of Christian Perfection in Early Methodism*

The Lives of the Saints and Other Poems took hold of my heart and imagination immediately. I have tended to feel that saints were (and are) perfectionists, individuals who achieved a closeness to God and a state of holiness far beyond my reach. However, Harris invites you to take a look at the real lives of saints: the messy, meager, weird, wild, brave, and beautiful souls who walked before, and still walk among us. The souls that dared to believe there is an adventure waiting for them and that this adventure is way too good to miss out on. Harris's poems not only give you a glimpse of these lives, they invite you right into the adventure with them. More importantly, Harris reminds us that we are all on the adventure of a lifetime and that you too, my friend, are a saint.

> Lyndsay Thompson, DMin, RP
> Lecturer in Counselling and Thanatology,
> Tyndale University

The Lives of the Saints

And Other Poems

Dale Harris

The Lives of the Saints and Other Poems
© 2025 by Dale Harris

DMH Books
PO Box 78003, Taunton Rd
Oshawa, Ontario, Canada
L1K 0H7

Cover illustration depicts the sixth-century Egyptian icon of Jesus with Saint Menas, commonly known as the icon of Jesus and his friend.
© 2017, Godong/Alamy Stock Photo. Used with permission.

ISBN 978-1-7777228-3-8

For Dani,
who is to me the most
beloved saint of all

Contents

Preface

I grew up in a staunchly evangelical faith tradition, where the only thing that really mattered in the spiritual life was one's personal relationship with Jesus, and anything that might complicate this relationship was treated with great suspicion, if not outright rejection. As a result, I was taught to hold anything that was even faintly redolent of Catholicism at a good arm's length. The Catholics don't have a personal relationship with Jesus (I was taught). Their relationship with God is mediated through an elaborate system of man-made rituals and traditions (so the rumor went). They don't believe you are saved by grace alone, through faith alone, in Christ alone. And worst of all, they pray to the saints (supposedly) because they think you have to go through them to get to God instead of talking to Jesus directly.

We read Hebrews 12:1 with the utmost of seriousness, but this was primarily because our beliefs about the inerrancy of Scripture required us to, not because we really thought that the faithful who had gone before were still surrounding us—in a way that might actually help us to run our own race well—with their great cloud of witness. We read Revelation 6:9 as literally as possible, with its vivid description of that great host of martyrs under the altar in heaven, crying out to the Almighty for justice on the earth. But this was not because we actually believed that they really had some intercessory influence, but only because we earnestly trusted Revelation as a literal account of how the world would end, and so by default, this verse, too, had to be true. We were far too interested in what Revelation might tell us about the timing of the Second Coming vis-à-vis the Great Tribulation, to give much consideration to this vision of the saints in heaven, praying for the saints on earth.

Even though this was the water I drank and the air I breathed in the religious environment I came of age in, still, I've always had a deep, if somewhat clandestine fascination with the stories of the Catholic saints. They just seemed so ancient and mystical, profoundly poetic, spiritually heroic, and especially (this was important to me even in the early days of my faith formation), compellingly beautiful. In an evangelical tradition like mine, we loved to point out that the word "saint"—God's *sanctified ones*—is a term the New Testament uses to describe all believers. We are all of us saints, in the biblical sense of the term, and as such, someone like Patrick of Ireland is no more or less a saint than anyone else. As a young Christian, I swallowed my medicine on this point, but even so, whenever I took the time to look into the lives of the saints (in the Catholic sense of the word), I couldn't escape the humbling sense that there was, in fact, a great deal of difference between me and someone like Francis of Assisi, say, or Thomas Aquinas, these giants of piety and devotion.

It wasn't until I was studying theology during my training for pastoral ministry that I began to come to terms with the half-truths and misrepresentations I had absorbed from the evangelical tradition of my childhood. As I did, I began to understand more clearly how the stories of the saints could speak to my own heart's ache for the same kind of spiritual adventure and vivid devotion as they embodied. A crucial turning point for me was reading Thomas Howard's *Evangelical is not Enough*, a sort of evangelical's guide to the historic liturgy of the Church. In a deceptively simple but profoundly wise passage, he provides this explanation of the Church's veneration of Mary—and it's a thought that can be stretched more generally to apply to all the saints:

> We are taught by Scripture that nothing may be *worshiped* but God alone. The ancient Church has always taught this, reserving for God alone the honor known as *latria*. But below this worship paid to the Most High, there is a whole scale of exultation and exaltation that rejoices in the plentitude of divine glory and leaps to hail every creature in whom that glory is seen.

In another passage, he explains the practice of asking the saints to pray for us, offering us the theological equivalence of some homespun common sense:

They are honored, and in some traditions their prayers are sought, not because Christ's intercessions on our behalf are not sufficient, but because He has made His whole church one with his intercessory ministry, so that, just as we ask one another here below for prayers, so we call upon those who have gone ahead of us and are more than ever part of this priestly Body of Christ.

Of course, the saints are not just extraordinary exemplars of world-changing devotion and other-worldly spirituality. They are also ordinary men and women like us, filled with their foibles, their self-doubts, their yearnings, and no less earthy or broken or wounded than we are (in many cases, far more so). This is another fascinating theme that threads through the stories of so many of the Church's saints, and especially those who have left us reliable biographical evidence of their lives. As much as they gave us glimpses of profound piety and near-supernatural self-sacrifice, still, they put their shoes on one foot at a time, the same way we do. In this sense, the evangelicals were right all along: we are all of us saints, no less than was Augustine or Teresa of Ávila. The fact that this is true, however, does not bring them down to our level, rather it ought to inspire us up toward theirs.

This is how I have come to think of them, anyways, as I have explored the stories of the saints more deeply. In reciting the Breastplate of Saint Patrick, I find myself compelled to resist this world's spiritual darkness with the same courage he once displayed; in praying the Prayer of Saint Francis, I find opening in my own heart the same channels of God's peace as coursed through his. And here I discover, perhaps, the deepest sense of what the Apostles' Creed had in mind, when it taught us to confess our belief, too, in the communion of the saints: the way the lives of the faithful who have gone before continue to inspire, inform, and bless our own lives as followers of Christ today.

It is in that spirit that I offer the poems in this book. Most of them were written during the Lenten season of 2025, when, as part of my Lenten journey, I committed to writing a poem each day until Easter. To give structure to this Lenten promise, I chose primarily to write poetic reflections based on the lives of the saints. Not every poem ended up being a saint poem. Some are more general reflections on my life as a pastor, a parent, a poet, a follower of Jesus, but even those that deal with other matters were still informed by the themes and imagery I kept encountering as I wrestled poetically with the lives of the saints. You can think of these non-saint pieces as simply the poetic shadows cast by their hagiographic light.

Some of the saints you will meet here have been life-long favorites of mine, especially St. Brendan the Navigator and Saint Patrick of Ireland. Some are so iconic as to be almost cliché, such as Saint Nicholas or Saint Valentine. Others I chose because they were so delightfully obscure, like Saint Nicholas Owen, the patron saint of stage magicians, or Saint Melangell, the patron saint of rabbits. I toyed with the idea of including a glossary with some guiding notes about which saint is which (how else would you know, for instance, that Saint Joseph is the patron saint of Canada, or Saint Hubert the patron saint of hunters?) In the end, however, I decided against this. Many times I have entered a Catholic cathedral and seen some beautiful statue or painting of some saint whose story I did not know. Rather than taking away from the aesthetic experience, however, I found that my ignorance in such moments only added a layer of mystery and wonder to it. Perhaps this might be something like your experience with some of the lesser-known figures in this collection.

But whether obscure or familiar, my hope is that through your encounters with the saints in these poems, you might find your own spiritual horizons expanding, your sanctified imagination being stirred, and new possibilities for the spiritual life opening in your heart. As you do, may you come to see with fresh eyes what it means for Christ to call all of us—with them—His saints.

April 25, 2025
Soli Deo Gloria

The Lives of the Saints

And just when you suppose you've seen it all,
Around the next unlikely corner comes
Some new devoted misfit or oddball,
Marching to the sacred beat of unheard drums:
Some swashbuckling and others mystical,
A shameless band of lovers and fanatics,
Dreamers waxing theological,
Those beautiful losers and hopeful romantics.
How strange that they should seem unusual,
Their reckless feats of faith and daring love,
When nothing could have been more natural
For spirits filled with fire from above:
And how I long to join that motley crew,
To find my humanness alive in You.

Whalefall

when   I am
gone   and
drifted to
the ocean
floor of
all my last
goodbyes,
when my
distended
legacy, like some
decaying corpse,
rich with   nurturing
dreams
discarded, their ribs
and purple entrails   stark,
exposed, and waving
freely in the
gentle current I
succumbed   to in the end—
when what I was and how I   lived has found its
final floating place,   slowly   turning in the
weightless   salt   dark:
may the rotting tatters
of that   disintegrating
whale flesh, my
heritage,   become a
haven, too, for all the
motley silver
fish I leave behind,
a feast and life-
support for those
to come,
a hide-
away
for silent
scuttling
claws

Eros and Psyche

In the back corner of a cluttered gallery
Of the Louvre's treasure trove
Stands, or rather swoons in ecstatic recline
The glorious marble embrace
Of Canova's *Eros and Psyche*.
Arching inward toward the other
Reaching, longing, lingering
For the tenderest of kisses never to touch,
Each gazes mesmerized eternally
Into the stone-still face of their beloved,
While iPhone-wielding tourists clatter past,
Hunting for trophied selfies with the smiling Mona Lisa.
Few if any, linger long enough to admire
How close they came to consummation,
Before the knowing of each other
Sent them spiraling apart forever.
The day I saw it,
Young and longing for my own Psyche
To awaken in the arms of its dear night-shrouded Eros
(To hold her gently in a pose so passionate
As to be almost painful)
I couldn't pull myself away;
And though the thought that I was seeing something
Even Psyche ought not have seen
Caught in my throat like shameful fire,
I stood and stared, rapt with wild wonder
And burning holy with desire.

Saint Ignatius

A thousand wounds in battle
Never cut so deep
Nor bled so fierce and free;
A thousand gaping guns
Never flashed so bright
Nor swords so piercingly
As one light touch
Of your pure hands upon the heart
Where love and risk burn singly,
One sole and yearning quest
For holy honors
And divine renown.

Nor could a thousand years
Of deepest rest
Provide such convalescence—
A thousand soothing balms
Never eased the soul
As does the luminescence
Of the healing rays
Of the rising sun
Of the glory of your presence:
For shining in that holy light
You have become my heart's campaign
And I your lover-knight.

Saint John of the Cross

But there was nothing good in that dark night,
Though never raging, nothing quiet in my soul
Or gentle in my striving for the light;

A hope was in the gloaming there, despite
The emptiness You hadn't yet made whole,
But there was nothing good in that dark night.

The untried heart might still naively fight
To catch a glimpse of something beautiful
Or gentle in my striving for the light,

But to the wise, or for the desperate,
Who've faced the silent black and gaping hole,
No: there was nothing good in that dark night;

Except—to this I cling with all my might—
The thought that I should find You merciful
Or gentle in my striving for the light:

For this I kneel, heart broken and contrite,
Inviting you to meet me and console—
Though there is nothing good in this dark night,
Or gentle in my striving for the light.

My David, Your Jonathan

If you would be my David
Then I'd be your Jonathan—
I would take off all the trappings
Of the glory I've got on;
And I'd remove my armor
And I'd offer you my crown,
If you would be a David
To my lonely Jonathan.

And I would stand before you,
Unclothed and without shame—
I would show you all my secrets
Just to hear you whispering my name;
And if it meant I could no longer
Be my father's son,
Still I'd let you be my David
If I knew that I could be your Jonathan.

(For there's a friend who still sticks closer
Than any brother could;
There's a water that is thicker
Than the purest drop of blood—
There is a love more wonderful
Than any I have known,
So hold me to your heart, my holy David
And I swear that I will be your Jonathan—
Yes: I swear that I will be.)

So when the night is lonely
And there's nowhere left to hide,
When I take my shot into the dark
Will you swear to never leave my side?
Or when my journey stumbles
And I've fallen on my sword,

If I swore to be your Jonathan
Would you swear with all your heart
To be my Lord?

Saint Teresa of Ávila

The agony of ecstasy: a flash
Of piercing joy and stab of healing fire
Embracing me and leaving in my flesh
The gaping wound of satisfied desire;
So quieted, I quail at the touch,
Your fingertips both soothe and burn—
The slightest brush with you is far too much
To bear, but not enough for how I yearn.
Thus blazing with angelic wings I find
A passion for pure passion in my soul.
I open to those hands that tear to bind
And feel an emptiness that leaves me whole;
O, make your bower in this heart you haunt,
Thou Love I fear, but want to want to want.

Saint Lucy

After the sudden stain of martyrdom
Has streaked its final crimson runnel down
My tearless cheek—after the light has flown
Like starlings startled from their roost and come
To rest in splatters on my pristine gown—
When I have wrapped myself in that thick shroud
Of utter dark and all-embracing cloud
And made these gaping eyes my saintly crown—
What visions then will burst upon my sight?
The rapture of those angel-throngéd skies
More radiant than any earthly light,
Unveiling Your concealed Majesty?
Ah! I would give far more than these my eyes
If You would give that glimpse of Life to me.

Saint Anastasia

A tortured soul shall be my salve,
This blood and bone my healing balm;
I break to feel my pain dissolve
Enfolded in His wounded palm—

And so with every gasping breath
I offer up my flesh to prove
How risen Life shines in my death,
My medicine His perfect love:

For as that physic burns to save,
A searing flash of sacred flame
Lights up the dark and empty grave
From which I take my martyr's name.

Saint Monica

But Mother Monica, you weren't the last
To offer up some deep maternal prayer
For a profligate son's unruly past,

Waiting up through long and sleepless nights
While he was gallivanting here and there
Until the debauched dawn of morning light;

And nor were you the first whose brooding soul
Was burdened with a mother's weight of care,
And wept to gather back her prodigal—

For the Spirit over primal waters wild
Was brooding like some restless momma bear,
Aroused by danger to protect her child:

And if in that First Vigil you've some share,
You'll find that Hell hath no brave challenger
As a mother knelt in unrelenting prayer.

Five Guitars

Once there were five guitars
Hanging on the wall,
Ready to pick up and play
When the Spirit came to call;
But three of them are packed up
And they're set out on the stage—
Once this house had five guitars
But three have come of age
(How quickly they all grew).
Once this house had five guitars
But now there's only two.

Abadigido
—for Rachael

How deeply I remember it,
That afternoon so long ago
When you took daddy by the hand
And told him, "abadigido."

You couldn't tell me what it meant;
You said you didn't know.
But never had you meant a word
Like you meant abadigido.

It was an open sesame
To mysteries you couldn't show,
A treasure trove of pure delight,
The password: abadigido.

'Cause Rosebud for the dying Kane,
Abracadabra, Code Bravo,
And Jabberwocks with eyes of flame—
All met in abadigido.

(Not even supercalafra-
galisticexpialido-
cious did the trick so easily
As saying abadigido.)

Like Jephthah with his shibboleth
To guard the Jordan River's flow,
It marked out who belonged to you
When you said abadigido.

Some things get buried by the years
And other things you just outgrow,
And daddy can't remember when
He last heard abadigido.

But when you find you need it most,
In voiceless joy or wordless woe
And you can't bear to bare your soul,
I pray it will return to you,
The wisdom that you always knew,
To look the world in the eye
And tell it, "abadigido."

On Lazy Days

I don't do well with lazy days.
The slouching silhouette of guilt
That lurks down the dark alley
Of all that idleness haunts even
My best efforts at languid luxury.
The rarest lazy day of all
Never brought the spender
Gilded, glorious works of art
Or sonorous symphonies celebrated
Or mysteries uncovered
Or any of these deepest longings
Of my heart that only blood and sweat
And unwept tears can buy.
Rather than spend them instead I'd invest
And live a fecund prodigal
Off the burgeoning interest of all those
Unspent lazy days.
         And so I have, and do,
Until the Holy Hand of the Eternal Word
Comes settling to rest,
Gentle and warm to still my every striving.
Not even Adam in Paradise, it seems to say,
Had to earn his unproductive Sabbath.
His only duty, on the first day of the rest of his life
Was to enjoy a precious holiday with You,
Beautifully wasted in a
State of holy languor.

Saint Nicholas Owen

In death-defying chains and daring locks
Houdini was in deepest need of prayer,
And Copperfield in his collapsing box,
Or Hermann snatching bullets from thin air—
With nothing up their sleeves and naked wrists,
Their beautiful assistance sawn in half,
These escape artists and illusionists
All needed saintly prayers on their behalf;
And who's to say, perhaps, but so do we:
For we all have illusions of our own,
Those secret tricks we can't let others see,
Without which we might know as we are known.
Thank God, He sees through our magician's art—
Our misdirecting souls and sleight of heart.

Saint Hubert

A glimpse of twisted antler
    Slipping silent through the gnarled branches
Draws my yearning onward
    In an empty-handed chase;

And as the skittish Hart of Heaven
    Skips a beat into the underbrush
I hunted, unaware I was
    The quarry of your grace.

But hind's feet in high places
    Coursing pathways through the shadowed valley
Lead me to a clearing
    Where the seeker is the sought;

And in that baptized vision
    Of the thorns that form your antler-crown
I grasp it in the catching
    That my hunted heart was caught.

Saint Christopher

And rumor has it that Saint Christopher
Was like some horrid cynocephalus—
A grim, dog-headed man named Reprobus
Before the infant Christ answered his prayer—
That dog-toothed smile of his instilling fear
In all and sundry passing by his way,
Until he bore the Holy Child one day
And Jesus made his human face appear.
Of course, it's just a legend, but how apt
A story for the saint of wayfarers:
For every pathway walked and journey mapped
Are signposts to the guiding One he bears,
Who leads us on a voyage wide and far,
Away from who we were and into who we are.

Saint Brendan the Navigator

And King of Mysteries, shall I then abandon
Home and country, kin and cradle-land
To trust myself into your unseen hand
And launch my currach into the unknown—
Shall I kneel here on the beach alone
And leave my prayer imprinted in the sand,
To push off from this fixed and foam-kissed strand
And be where wave will wash and wind has blown?
For if in the battering wounds of the sea
Or the sting of salted foam on furrowed brow,
If drifting like some landless albatross
I find that you have not forsaken me,
I'll make my empty tomb this cresting bow
And all these wild waves my carried cross.

Saint Bernard

Such   a
shame   your
long and   storied
legacy should   be reduced to
cartoon images of   blind and brandy-
bearing dogs, bounding   through snow after
hapless skiers have taken   their ridiculous spills, when
His high and treacherous calling: the rescue of waylaid pilgrims
with warm hearths and hot baths to   ease their travel-stained hearts
(not to mention the risk of dignifying the   deaths of those who slipped)
was no light or laughing matter. For who   among us hasn't once looked
down with reeling vertigo and almost   lost their footing? And how holy were
those hands (of His) that reached   out just in time to steady us and help us
find our narrow Way, up the   sheer ascent and over that final waiting ridge?

Sailing the Sea of Tranquility

We push away under star dappled skies
As the silver sirens sing their sweet lullabies
And the iridescent flying fish harmonize;
O, they dance in the wake as our crystalline ship passes by.

And moondust mermaids point the way through the night
While the dolphins give chase in the mystical light,
And the starfish and glofish are all shining bright—
Sailing on for the country of perfect unearthly delight.

    Sailing, sailing, where no breezes blow.
    Sailing, sailing, on waves of pure shalom.
    In the haven of your heart I can float,
        It's zero gravity;
    We're sailing, sailing, on the Sea of Tranquility.

A crescent earth shines like a blue scimitar,
Burning bright overhead, it's become our lodestar,
And the tide flowing in from the sea of nectar
Carries us on our way through the dark to the heavenly shore.

    Sailing, sailing, for that mystical land.
    Sailing, sailing, guided by your hand.
    In the haven of your heart I discover
        I'm one with my destiny;
    We're sailing, sailing, on the Sea of Tranquility.

Scintillating beneath the celestial dome
Far beyond where the lunar leviathan roams,
Where the beaches are gilded with glittering foam,
We arrive on the shimmering sands of our celestial home.

Saint Patrick

Invoking faith and bound with Trinity,
In morning's twilit grey I would arise
To sanctify my vision with your eyes
And see the thing that only you can see;
And yet, I fear the path you've laid for me:
On moor and over parting seas it lies,
Through fen and under raven-darkened skies
Back to the land of my captivity.
So: like the carved and woven braids of stone,
Those snaking strands that form the Celtic cross,
Would you entwine your Spirit with my bone
Until I fear no death nor any loss?
Thus armed with you and one with my desire
I'll light the Hill of Slane with paschal fire.

Saint Nicholas

I have no doubt that you were jovial
Or festive in the truest sense of all
Those weary words, but there (no doubt)
The sorry simulacra stops.

For tremulous, that Jove-like joy of yours—
The feast that you were getting ready for—
Was nothing we could package or adorn
To buy and sell in shops;

And every ringing bell and star-topped tree
At best is but a shady parody
Of that resplendent Life, more wonderful
Than all our tired Christmas tropes,

And even the most glittering of lights
On our most frigid winter nights
Can barely hint at how that Child's coming
Quieted our fears and answered all our hopes.

The War on Christmas

The warriors are out in force tonight
With Merry Christmas as their battle cry,
Their reasons for the season ringing high
Above the glittering noise and blaring lights;
Insisting "all is calm," they keep things bright
With gilded trees and songs of angels in the sky,
Proclaiming all the products you can buy
To laud the Child and so protect our rights.
And who's to say a battle's not at hand
To steal the Christ from underneath the tree?
For when he's gone perhaps we'll understand
How nothing could be more like Calvary
Than winning the war on Christmas forever
By quietly losing it altogether.

A Pastor Musing in His Study

How much pain there would be
If every Sunday felt the pressure
Of a Christmas Sunday,
To get the words just so and the
Worship all in perfect order,
So that every last drop of the wonder
Of God's Love come down to us
In the Gift of Immanuel,
Wrapped squirming in a manger
Might be savored?

How much pain,
But oh how much the pleasure?

Saint Valentine

But somewhere far beneath
the gaudy clutter of those
heart-shaped trinkets lingers—
lost in all the silly crimson
wrappings, still—the faintest echo
of your ancient, faithful witness;
O, Martyr of Marriage, remind us again
that no self-offering is trivial
and every gift (however trite) is precious
when it's offered as a mirror
of the Lord who gave his very life
to keep His covenant
(but also He who taught us that
our faithfulness in little things
is faithfulness in great, and the
everyday is actually
the stuff of sacrifice).
For maybe somewhere in
the garish remnants of your memory
I'll learn from Him (through you)
and make my faithful marrying
a simple witness, too.

The Birds and the Bees

In the stairwell hangs a print
Of that obscure Pre-Raphaelite:
A mercilessly belle and fragrant dame,
Open mouth and face alight,
Entwining in the tresses
Of her intoxicating hair
The broad, enchanted shoulders
Of her captive knight.

I might have fallen for her, too,
Except I know the ending:
How those fey, fell eyes,
So wild and so ravishing
Will leave him; and because I do
(And have) I almost—well—
I pity her, who has a longing
Of her own, a burning fire
No less warm than mine, but for which she
Must hang (not me), a warning dire:
That in the end all birds must die
However beautifully they sing—
And sweet as is the honey, still
Every bee must sting.

On First Reading Jewel, ca. 1998

Like a Don Juan
    who couldn't get it
up
are my idle vaults at
    philosophy and art.

For after so much
    fruitless putting
out
to find myself
    spent—
           died—
               and yet not—
come,

(the lover soft & condescending
accentuating the shame)

is to be—
    bitterly flaccid—
in so much yearning desire.

Saint Columba

No less than Milton, Saint Columba, too,
Thou shouldst be living at this waning hour,
For never have we had such need of you
As now: our weary hearts have lost the power
To feel the savored sting of well-wrought words
And our neglected poets stand on trial,
Their wrestling pens far weaker than the swords
Of certainty that threaten their exile—
But when they're gone then who will help us see
The Grace that we could never understand
Without their mystic ambiguity?
We're blind to it, and we don't even know it,
For there's no one left to take a stand
And speak up for the heart-work of the poet.

Saint Cecilia

O, Cecilia, you're mending my heart
And shaping my devotion in the sweet
Soft strains of songs set silently apart
Like broken perfume poured out at his feet.
Not even three swift strokes of two-edged swords
Could pierce a martyr's soul so perfectly
As does a single note more pure than words
Resolving in your virgin melody;
Nor could they separate your heart and head—
Your cadences together kept them bound,
And even after they had left you dead
Your soul still sang, celestial the sound.
So I discover, when I sing along:
The real tribulation is the song.

Sometimes

I've learned it's always better
Not to measure tasks
    By what you want to do
        But by the things you want
           To have had done.
Which is why the taking up of pen and page
Is still such joyous agony for me—
    Despite the weight of finding that
        First Word,
So strived for and so unexpected,
And the straining, herculean heave
        Of setting it down in ink.
    Sometimes the inertia summons
        All my heart, soul, mind
           And strength to overcome
(So much, at times,
As to feel overwhelming);
Yet, for the sake of that
        Sudden flash of clarity,
The glimpsing of some hidden side of You
That no one could have otherwise imagined,
    It is infinitely worth all this
        And more—
Not for the joy of the doing
(Though that, at times, does still break through)
    But for the sheer delight
    Of all the things that,
        Had I never done,
           Never would
               Have been.

Saint Chrysostom

You silver tongued devil, you, how suave
You are, with metaphors of milk and honey
Guiding us through deserts dry and stony,
Leading to a Promised Land of Love;
For so with whispered joy and holy dread,
You'd weave your awe-inspired tapestry:
Your trembling loom His sacred Mystery,
Unspeakable delight its golden thread—
But tongue-tied by the wondrous News you've heard,
Like Balaam's ass you merely bray and bleat,
Struck dumb and desperate for the Living Word
To stoop and beautify those ugly feet:
That he might speak His Spirit through your soul,
You cauterize your lips with flaming coal.

An Epiphany

As pastor I am the forgotten crayon
Shoved into the front pocket
Of the congregational pair of blue jeans,
Chucked haphazardly into
The laundry machine of Church Life.

If I am pink the whites will all turn rose.
If I am green, they'll come out a sickly hue.
If I am yellow, then yellow will become the clothes;
If grey, eventually they'll turn a faded blue.

On Speaking Up

Constantly risking absurdity or death,
Said Ferlinghetti about the poet's speaking up;
And yet weekly I walk a half-hour
Tight rope strung taut between
The twin poles of divine transcendence
And human immanence,
An absurd dying and rebirthing
That is no real risk but a lived reality,
Where everything and nothing is on the line.
This is my speaking up
In the face of apathy to things divine,
The disenchantment of the universe,
Blindness to the prevenience of grace
And the weary human capitulation
To every oppressor: sin and death and devil.
I know at any moment the crowd
Might snap awake and hear far more than I am saying,
And God knows what hell might break loose then—
What demons defeated—
What wounds healed—
What raging waves stilled—
What burning questions fanned into flame?
The only fear greater than the fear of this
Is the fear of saying nothing at all.

Proof of Concept

I don't believe
I've ever seen
The promised harmony
Of earth and heaven,
Joined as one
And distilled down
Into a holding hand
Or inclined ear,
The lingering embrace
Of a long-awaited friend.
I've never seen
Our flesh and bone
Transcending space and time
And hurt and healing,
Breath and soul,
And all this weary world
With its rumors of a heart made whole.
I've never seen,
But I believe
That in your passing
By and through
And over me,
In tongues of flame
And sacred pledges kept,
That even though I've never seen,
At least I have
The proof of concept.

Saint Albert the Great

Teach me the Fingerprints of God,
O, teach me:
      big bangs and
      flying matter outward
      inward,
      swirling nebulae of cosmic dust to
      centres larger than the whole and
      gravity anchoring planets to their
      seven singing spheres their
      orbits,
      pulling everything that must go up
      down and into centres,
      new centres;
      O, teach me all centres!
      the most intricate workings
      of the matter He ordained;
      teach me of electrons in
      quantum motion about
      their protons and their neutrons,
      and the smallest, thinnest, strongest bonds
      of perfect love divine,
      and the constitution of positive and negative,
      of equal and opposite reactions,
      of burgeoning light and call them photons,
      of fissions and fissions and
      super-novas of fissions until—
      a fusion,
      a solar fusion,
      a blossoming of gravity and light and matter,
      the earth and water, air and fire ordered,
      arrayed in perfect order
      and all the other elements,
      in perfect hierarchy:
      hydrogen the first to
      radium, uranium, plutonium,

their numbers and charges
and masses of matter
ordered by gravity from chaos;
Yes! Teach me chaos,
The old familiar tear never sliding
the same trail
down the rough-fleshed cheek,
and random ions spinning nebulaic
into webs of images:
ooze, or dust, or primal life,
primordial images—
Yes, teach me those images!
Those cells selected by divine command,
kissed blushing with His breath:
to grow and shape,
revolve, evolve,
array and multiply, array
and multiply, array and multiply until—
life, teach me
new life:
the strange unearthly creation reaching
neonate from the water, reaching
firstborn from the darkness,
reaching out and;
teach me of changes!
of changing creatures,
changing creation,
of climates cyclical rising and falling,
of crashing continents
and great shifting palms of earth sliding,
of retreating seas and
jungles fecund and advancing,
of endless cycles of kingdoms and phyla
and classes and orders,
of undulating genera
and species—
teach me too of species!
of biology and botany,
of broad and sultry fronds

spreading mighty through the air,
spreading, throbbing, primal forests,
coursing green with blood;
and of zoology:
the endless parade
of the pleasures of divine imagination,
and teach me, too, of that breath-breathed-dust,
of bare, forked creatures rising slowly
through the ages,
stepping forward through their eons,
stepping up to stand
at that sudden, spoken instant of creation!
Yes! teach me!
of humours and ichor, of bile and mucus
and all the combinations of hot and dry
and cold and wet that course about
anatomy,
of egos and ids, of animus and anima,
the holy flame that draws me
to the rough-fleshed body
of another,
new gravities, but old,
the bright white flash that joins two cells!
that joins and yet divides them!
of genes and DNA to organize their chaos,
and the intricate workings of the
matter you ordained:
electrons coursing through the blood and ions
of that new-conceived soul,
dividing and joining, dividing and joining,
dividing until—
that final, laborious division,
clinging yet by a long and narrow
tube of life, divided
and yet searching;
O, teach me all searchings!
every understanding and discovery,
every exploration and compassion,
everything there is to know

about His good and enigmatic
Universe.

Yet know
     that this
          is not God.
For even the rose,
by any other name
Would always be
     glucose and
     sucrose and
     photosynthesis,
     that innumerable array
     of green and pink
          cells stacked neatly
               and ordered—
but still eternally more
than the sum of all those parts.

So knowing God's Ways and Means,
does not reduce,
rather expands God infinitely
within the weak reason,
     the too-thin logic
          of our mortal minds,
     accommodating the immortal, invisible
          God Only Wise—
as God fans the flame of wonder
into the limited dimensions,
     of the feeblest anatomy
          of our meek and awe-struck hearts.

An Analogy

Poles pull together
Only when their difference
Attracts them to each other,
When positive can fill
The void of negative,
And negative is faced
The proper way.

But when they are alike
(Or trying to be so)
When negative is turned
And pretending to be full—
A simple fact of nature is
That positive can only push
A positive away.

And so it is between
That Perfect Love Divine and me:
When I admit that It is All
And everything I'll never be,
It draws me to the centre of
Its Sacred Heart;

But when I turn and make myself
The other pulling pole—
And stand as positive as though
We were somehow equal,
Then It becomes unyielding Force
And I'm repelled (or I repulse)
Inevitably pushing us apart.

Saint Thomas Aquinas

Oh Tom, you big dumb ox
With your wheelbarrow full of books!
As if we could somehow define
The specs of the divine.

Your Mover First Unmoved
Could never fathom how He loved,
Nor could mere Natural Law express
The scandal of His grace.

Thank God eternity
Waits patiently for you (and me)
With time enough to pick apart
The *summa* of His heart.

Leda and the Swan Revisited

Only now the swan's become
An eagle clutching wildly
And flexing spangled talons
While he snatches Leda unprovoked
From her peaceful place
Among the crimson maple boughs;
And Zeus the great and languid
Is a small and bloated man,
Grabbing her by more than just her virgin neck
With his rapacious appetite
And soulless lechery.

Saint Joseph

And Joseph, son of David,
    Though you bit your tongue
    With swallowed pride
The day that you adopted
    Mary's sacred little One

Remember this, your patronage,
    Our humble home and
    Native land
The next time that you're talking
    With your Holy Foster Son;

For we are at the dawning of
    An age of monstrous cruelty,
    And nothing but His grace
Can keep us glorious
    And free,

So in your humble yes to Him
    Teach us to welcome
    In his reign
And give His love dominion from sea
    To sea to sea.

Saint Adrian

O, patron saint of arms dealers
  Pray for us,
While all our hungry pruning hooks
Get beaten into javelins
And all our precious plowshares
  Into swords.

They say the day He conquered you,
  You asked them—
All those faithful, tortured souls
Whose martyrdom you supervised—
What made them so devoted
  To their executed Lord?

O, from the promised answer that they
  Offered you,
That vision of a coming day
No weeping eye has ever seen
Nor aching prophet's ear has
  Fully heard,

Please pray for us, our patron saint
  Of paradox.
For savage wolves still roam the earth
Devouring the Slaughtered Lamb—
And tempting us to trade for bombs
  His beatific word.

Good Sport

I'm not so much
A fan of hockey,
But they say
We won last night.

And as they do, my son
Points out to me
That when our team
Wins we say, "We won."
But when they don't
We say, "They lost."

As in: "They lost
Last Sunday night."

Again, I'm not so much
A fan of hockey,
But I wonder if there isn't
Some ancient glimpse
Of Adam's sin,
Hidden in that
Unnoticed tendency of ours
To include
(only when we gain from it)
Those we decisively will exclude
When we find they can't deliver.

Saint Martin de Porres

But other dreamers
will come,
hopeful Martin,
wearing your wild notions
    of siblinghood
    on their defiant sleeves—
        setting out the shalom-shaped dish
        you scoured first with your
        blood and sweat and tears
    and welcoming us all
    to its earthenware lip:
        mice and hound and hunting
        cat—lion and lamb—
            adder and child,
        eating together as one.
Not that we will
heed them any better
when they do,
    snatching the plate to ourselves
    with gluttonous claws,
        scurrying off the mice
        and refusing to eat
        so long as the dog is there.
O, pray for us!
And for all of these
your namesakes—
    who continue to summon us back
    with their prophetic dreams,
    to take our place among them all
    at His too-humble feast—
that we might still retain
our undeserved seat
    (among the nibbling mice
    and gently-coiled snakes)
        when at last the Table becomes

a mercifully-anchored,
(but still, for all that)
a justice-founded
    Throne.

Saint Moses the Ethiopian

For a lifetime of imaging Him
As some Swedish Adonis
I'm sorry—
For no christ so pale as he
Could ever have saved
A heart like yours,
Brimming reckless with adventure
And longing to tip things upside-down—
No blue-sashed,
Privileged messiah
Could have caught and held
That unbridled affection
And brazen devotion
The way it needed His embrace,
Or drawn you, sword in teeth
Across the Nile and deep into
The Wadi's lonely wastes;
And neither could it me,
Though I never fully realized
Until we met:
That if I'm going to be saved
It would have to be a Christ
As black as you—
Or at the very least
Not near so white
As me.

Saint Kateri Tekakwitha

And what would you have thought,
 Saint Tekakwitha, I wonder,
  With your baptized eyes
   Would you have seen
  The things I thought I saw
In that pitch and pressing dark,
  Dripping wet with prayerful agony,
   While drumming throbbed
   And rattles shook
  And litanies were offered up
   To thank and stir Creator?
Would you have deigned to take a place
 Amid that close and pressing circle,
  Making His that medicine
   You long had left behind?
Though you belonged as tribe and kin
 Where I was but a cautious guest,
  Would you have raised your voice to sing,
   Your moccasins removed as if
  You stood on holy ground?
If so, what would your prayer have been:
 That we might be redeemed, or it?
  In the earth-womb of that sweating lodge,
   Would you have asked Creator God
  To hear and bless our liturgy,
   Or mercifully forgive?

Saint Dympha

Even in my wildest dreams
    I couldn't have imagined
        Gentle Dympha on the Judgement Day,
        Serenely standing with our Lord;
And all her sibling-children gathered round:
    The broken and unsettled souls
    She'd prayed for since her parting
        Taking shelter in the haven of that
    Safe and tender side—
Where they sit,
All clothed and in their right minds,
Having stripped off every label:
    All those bedlamites and lunatics,
        The madmen, raving maniacs,
            Psychotics, schizophrenics
                With their misplaced marbles found.
They've wandered in from east and west,
    From borderlines and hedgerows,
        Welcomed in to take their tranquil place
        At that Final Feast of Fools.
I really can't imagine, but I see:
    And how I think I'd long to join her
        (For King Lear is there, I'm sure,
        And so is Van Gogh, maybe Mozart)
Yet my neat and tidy reasons,
    Pristine answers *sans* remainder—
        My *cogito ergo sum*
Makes of me the awkward misfit,
    As I try to set things right-side-up
        And know I don't belong.

Saint Agatha of Sicily

I was not there the day those cruel pincers tore
Your faithful flesh; those weren't my hands that ripped
To tattered shreds the vestal dress you wore,
Your exposed breasts like helpless dove wings clipped;
Nor could I groan the way you must have groaned
As heartless iron cut and bruised and pricked
In places I could never be, a wound
I cannot know, but only could inflict.
Yet even though the blame's not mine to bear
I long to offer my apology,
For in that hurt I know I have some share,
As I am heir to that dark legacy—
And even Christ could know what you went through
Only because He suffered there in you.

Saint Sebastian

Of course, they never would have canonized
The likes of you, if anyone had guessed
At who your patronage would come to bless,
Or what your yearning body symbolized,
Those torturous and arrow-piercéd thighs
A mark of both your torment and your bliss,
Like lovers stealing that forbidden kiss
So many since have seen there in your eyes.
If only they could feel your agony,
Who judge at scars but never felt a wound,
Or know the gaping need with which it streamed,
The pain of unrequited ecstasy.
For it embraced the ones we had disowned,
That all our misfit loves might be redeemed.

The Telling of the Bees

When all the bees at last are gone
To whom will we confess
The grief we feel
At their so sudden leaving—
The heartache of our unkissed blossoms,
All our barren limbs and fruitless buds?
Who will hear our whispered yearning,
How we miss their summer humming?
Who will know our heart's desire
For the taste of honey on our tongues?
And who will help us find our way
Up from the Stygian shore of winter,
Out into the light of a new spring sun?
Who will hear our dying woes,
When light is gone and earth is cold?
To whom will we confess our sins
When everything is come undone
And all the listening bees
At last are gone?

Saint Melangell

Small miracles: that, quivering,
    This hunted, heart-shaped mass
Should find its sanctuary underneath
    Your homespun dress,

Its warren in your tender lap,
    Its briars your tangled hair:
For when the hounds came hunting round,
    Their trail ended there.

But what petition did you make
    To make its Maker heed
That soft and trembling woodland life
    Alone in naked need?

Those long and cow'ring ears pulled back
    Eyes wide and fugitive—
Perhaps you saw yourself in it,
    And prayed you both might live.

For you were no less desperate,
    Your eyes were just as wild
As was that sylvan soul you had
    Adopted as your child,

And in your love for God's green earth,
    All creatures, rough or quaint
You made that delicate embrace
    The calling of a saint.

Saint Francis of Assisi

When everyone is finally
Together for that family
Reunion on that last and raucous Day,

I hope I'll find I'm sitting there
In easy earshot of your chair,
As all the revelry gets underway.

For Master Sun and Lady Moon
Will be reclining there with you
And Brother Water, bright and pure and clear,

And all the brother birds you knew—
The ones you sang the Gospel to—
And all your sisters: cow and cloud and deer

(And even Brother Fire might
Stop by to give you back the sight
He borrowed when you needed it the least).

And best of all, old Brother Ass—
Though how he got there I can't guess—
The tired flesh you rode here to the feast.

But then a holy hush will fall,
And someone in the crowd will call
To hear the Savior's dashing minstrel sing;

How sweetly you'll take up the song
(If only I could sing along)
Till all the heav'nly rafters start to ring:

The well-known ballad that you lived,
On loving more than you are loved
And seeking not to be known but to know,

And bringing hope where there's despair,
Or unity when hatred's there,
And sowing seeds of mercy as you go.

Although, there'll be new verses, too,
A coda that we never knew,
Reminding us that channels never start

Unless the water's faithful wear—
Or loss and pain—has carved them there
Like deep stigmata gouged into the heart.

So when we all are finally
In-gathered for that family
Reunion on that New and raucous Day,

I hope I'll get to hear that song
(Perhaps I'd dare to sing along)
As all the revelry gets underway.

Pentecost Sunday

Has
it really
been but
fifty short days?
To me it seems a
lifetime—catching
you just fleeting
round doorways and
out of the corners of
eyes—springing up in
bubbling moments of
freedom or contentment—
but dissipating, vaporous,
before the Dove can finally,
fully alight. Like snow held hot
in clenched and earnest fists, no
sooner (it seems) do I hold you—
or let you me—than it's gone (though
not without leaving its mark). Fifty years
(not days?) of waiting for the wind to roar,
the walls to shake, the fire to fall—and
yet I'm waiting still, breathing deep
your beauty, exhaling your grace,
and circling you, enraptured,
like a flitting moth drawn
desperately to warm
and sacred
flame.

About the Author

Dale Harris is a poet, novelist, songwriter, and ordained minister living in Oshawa, Ontario. He holds an M.Div from Briercrest Seminary (Caronport, SK) and a D.Min from Northeastern Seminary (Rochester, NY). Through his writing he loves to explore the spiritual dimensions of everyday things and the mysterious presence of God in both the bright and dark seasons of life. His other books include: *A Feast of Epiphanies, Daytime Moons and Other Celestial Anomalies*, and *Though I Walk* (winner of the 2021 Braun Book Award for fiction). He is the creator of Three Minute Theology, a YouTube channel that imaginatively explores the central doctrines of the Christian Faith. He can be contacted through his blog: daleblogging.blogspot.ca.

www.ingramcontent.com/pod-product-compliance
Lightning Source LLC
Chambersburg PA
CBHW032053040426
42449CB00007B/1091